The Path of a Rosicrucian Meditant

The Path of a Rosicrucian Meditant

Paintings by Ehrenfried Pfeiffer
Commentary by Paul W. Scharff, M.D.

Mercury Press

Paintings by Ehrenfried Pfeiffer
Text by Paul W. Scharff, M.D.

ISBN: 978-1-957569-08-6
Cover painting detail by Ehrenfried Pfeiffer

Published in the USA by
MERCURY PRESS
an imprint of SteinerBooks
PO Box 58
Hudson, NY 12534
www.steinerbooks.org

Printed in the United States of America

Helpers on the Way

There are several people that need to be recognized for their contributions in bringing this spiritually significant and historically important book project to fruition.

It is through Paul and Ann Scharff's iniative to gather and care for these paintings that they now form a permanent collection making this book project possible.

Marie G. Bruno of Arte Artiganato Restauro Inc. completed the careful restoration and conservation of the paintings.

Ben Caswell of Ben Caswell Photography photographed the paintings for inclusion in this book.

Anne Nicholson designed the book layout and made certain that the reproduced images were consistent with the paintings.

Carol O'Brien volunteered her services to transcribe the recorded talks Paul Scharff gave on the paintings. Ann Scharff edited the transcriptions for continuity and clarity.

Harold Bush coordinated the efforts of those involved so that the many parts could come together.

Mercury Press culminated these efforts with the publication, printing, and binding of *The Path of a Rosicrucian Meditant.*

Introduction

The material presented here, both the introduction as well as the comments regarding each picture, was compiled from two informal presentations by Dr. Paul Scharff given to individuals interested in Ehrenfried Pfeiffer and his life work. The material has been edited to the extent that appropriate portions of each presentation have been combined so that aspects of each painting are as broadly represented as possible from Dr. Scharff's perceptions.

The short biography of Ehrenfried Pfeiffer, which he gave at the beginning, was a sharing of some aspects of his life in acquainting those present with a little background. Anyone wishing to know more about the life of Ehrenfried Pfeiffer can find further material in the book *Ehrenfried Pfeiffer, A Modern Quest for the Spirit*, compiled and introduced by Thomas Meyer, translated by Henry Goulden and published by Mercury Press.

Text for the Pfeiffer Paintings

Ehrenfried Pfeiffer was born in 1899, at the end of the Kali Yuga and the beginning of the time of light. He died in 1961. He found his connection to Rudolf Steiner at the time when he went to a lecture by Rudolf Steiner in a factory in Germany. He was in the audience. This lecture took place in a beer garden and everyone in the audience was having a drink. Steiner's mouth was dry as he was trying to give the talk. Pfeiffer had sympathy, got up and got Rudolf Steiner a glass of water. At that moment a connection was made between them. He then became a rather personal pupil and was given material that Rudolf Steiner shared with him. Pfeiffer was a young man of 19 when Rudolf Steiner brought him to Dornach and assigned him the task of doing the lighting work in the First Goetheanum. This was to the dismay of many of the older workers. He was working with a lot of mature individuals, skilled workmen, and they were not at all happy having a young chap like that around, being looked after by Rudolf Steiner. He was quite youthful and was an outspoken individual.

Rudolf Steiner was kind of a fatherly individual to him, but in no small way. He directed Pfeiffer's studies when he went later to get his degree at the University in Basel. He had to give a six-week summary of the content of every course and then an in-depth description of the teacher. Rudolf Steiner did not want that the learning was just a dead thing and asked that one should know who was speaking.

Pfeiffer went through his training in the university and had to touch many subjects – world economy, geography, geology, chemistry, world history, social history. You name it; he had to go through an immense breadth in his educational experiences.

He was not an easy person. He didn't mince words. When Pfeiffer was a child, Rudolf Steiner advised his mother to give him into the care of his grandparents because she could not get along with him. That was also true of numerous people; they could not get along with him, but he was really quite an exceptional individual, very sensitive, played the piano and had perfect pitch. He also had a bit of an inner eye for the elemental beings in nature, for the spiritual world. He often sensed things that others did not. When somebody is sensitive to that area of existence one is often sensitive to things in others that rub one a bit. And he was rubbed, and he didn't just take it complacently. Nonetheless, he didn't lack for respect or friends. With a friend, they started the research laboratory in Dornach.

He then came here to America in the thirties and earned his honorary MD degree for crystallization research work done at the Hahnemann Medical College in Philadelphia, Pennsylvania. After that he became responsible to the Myrin farm in Kimberton, PA. The farm is now known as the Camphill Kimberton Farm. He gave courses in Bio-Dynamic Agriculture in 1929-1930 for which we have some of the records. These very early courses that he gave, actually I would say, fathered the organic natural food movement in this country. You would not know that but the people that came out in the open and made the movement known, had taken courses by Pfeiffer at Kimberton. One was Rodale. This whole group of individuals interested in the organic movement started with Pfeiffer.

He remained at Kimberton for a while, but then things got difficult there. With that, he and his wife, Adelheid, moved to Chester, New York and started their farm. All this time he was writing. I once asked his wife when she had written the article she did about some recipes, and she said she didn't. "It was my husband." He was incredibly prolific. He did so much writing and so much work. Two young people from Dornach recently came to the United States and while here copied 9,000 pages of materials that I have collected from his laboratory or what came over from his laboratory. Pfeiffer was one of these individuals who didn't require a lot of sleep.

In the forties, he became ill with tuberculosis and was taken up at the Rockland County Sanitarium or what is now called the Robert Yeager Health Center. Dr. Robert Yeager cared for him. I would say Robert was a tremendously compassionate individual. That is why they named the center after him. He lived his life there and he really looked after people. Pfeiffer was one of them who was there and cared for over a number of years. Dr. Yeager gave him permission to do research work in the lab while he was there. He did some quite interesting original work with antitubercular drugs. But then he also did other research. He did comparative studies from, I think it was 7,000 - 6,000 BC until the 1920s, comparing politics, economics, religion and philosophy placing on one side what Rudolf Steiner had to say about whom and what he investigated. On the other side was what history told. I have the roll: a chart about twenty-five feet long. It is quite a work.

He made charts galore. Rudolf Steiner had recommended that he make diagrams and charts. He destroyed them as fast as he made them. While ill, he did a lot of reading and Erika Sabarth brought in books by the tons. You would be amazed at the extent to which he read.

Dr. Yeager came to love Pfeiffer very much. At his funeral, I have to say about my Anthroposophical colleagues, it was very interesting what they said. But when Yeager spoke, you really could hear the heart of a person who dearly loved the person he cared for.

These paintings I want to talk about were done when Pfeiffer was at the Sanatorium recovering from tuberculosis. So it is an expression of the soul life of somebody recovering from illness but speaks to a soul life that is highly unusual. He gave them out to different people. I don't know whether he explained any of what he had been doing to those whom he gave these pictures, but I never heard a word from him. They all came to me after he died when various individuals gave me the paintings. Now I have about twenty that are in the series I will show. There are others I have that are not included in this group. Imagine doing these paintings while one is ill. Also interestingly, Rudolf Steiner pointed out that much of our artisticness will be lost in time when tuberculosis would no longer be a major illness. Tuberculosis needs an artist. I take it tubercular people, paralytic people.

I would say that what you will see here in pictures are the meditant, the person that meditates, that is trying to make the transition from his experience of meditation through something that is pictorial and explainable in the usual world. So what you will see are his efforts to paint different archangelic beings and different elemental beings. What I would say is that it is not unusual for a meditant to try to translate his meditative experiences into pictures. Albert Steffen was another person that did this and others have done it also. It is very different than beings like we are here, one could say "enclosed". That is the manifestation of spiritual beingness in meditative consciousness and then its translation into pictures of something, yet different.

These pictures were collected over a ten-year period. I just lived with them when I got them one by one. I really didn't quite know how to work with them. Gradually it dawned on me that if one is to consider them, it would be to consider that a person is a Rosicrucian meditant and that he is trying to make his way through the hierarchies to the Seraphim and the Cherubim that you hear of at the gate of Paradise if you read the Old Testament. Remember, these are my interpretations; it is not what he said.

- Paul W. Scharff, M.D.

Paintings and Comments

Painting 1

I will start by showing a picture of a young man; I would say a meditant. Instead of having a halo, Pfeiffer painted a picture of a young man where the young man gets outside of his head. I can say he kind of breaks open his head so that he begins to perceive with a field around him, an etheric field, which he is sensitive to. This is a powerful picture of such a young meditating individual. This kind of yellow halo you would see in the Middle Ages as the halos of the saints, the people who perceive things, who were considered a bit developed. This is not the Middle Ages: this is modern man, trying to, as it were, find his way, could be her way, to the spiritual world. So I would say that this is a picture of a meditant. (In response to a question from the audience, Dr. Scharff said, "Yes, you could say that, it looks a bit like a Johannes from the Mystery Dramas.")

Painting 2

The next picture is a picture that I have always said is Ronceval. It is around Ronceval or in that area of the Pyrennes. It is a quite well known mystery center where numerous leading individuals were active, including teachers from the School of Chartres which, as you know in the Middle Ages, was probably the beginning of what we have now as liberal arts education. The School of Athens was, in a way, transported to Chartres and many of the people traveled from Chartres to a center in Spain. I cannot remember the name at the moment, but it is a very famous center. There was a continual exchange between Paris - Chartres and this center. in Spain. As you know, it was in the Middle Ages that Spain had its glory – Portugal and Spain – and the Islamic, Hebrew and Christian religious individuals were busy. What they were busy with you just can't believe. I mean they had a tremendous school of learning there. We have not really heard the last of what went on at that time.

This is a picture of that setting that Pfeiffer visited and then painted. Erika Sabarth always had it hanging in the Pfeiffer Laboratory. I liked always to see it there because that was their goal, a Rosicrucian laboratory. I would say a modern chemistry, a modern alchemy.

Painting 3

This next one I would say is the path from the depths of earth through the waters, through the depths of the earth to the heights of the sun. That is the earth-sun and the sun-sun. The searchers on the Rosicrucian path were always searching for the sun nature on earth. One can say, as Hermes sought the Osiris Sun nature, Moses sought the Moon nature with Jehovah. And what you have here of the Jehovah element is more the earthly element which then leads to its depth and this waterfall or whatever it is that one descends with the waters into the depths of the earth. You can say that sanctifies the earth with Sun and the Jehovah nature, which is kind of a leading direction in a meditative effort.

Painting 4

I would call this a picture of the Rosicrucian island of the soul in Rosicrucian meditation. You see the body of water. You see the quietness, the nature around one. The island is where the soul, the meditative soul, lives and the lake is quiet. It hides the watery wisdom that has to be in the world in order that we have transformation of the earth in chemical processes. I would say, contemplate this picture, and anybody that has tried to get to the island or creates them in his soul, will know how difficult it is to manage that acquisition.

Painting 5

I would say this is a rainbow bridge. It is also the bridge that Werner Glas had in mind when he named the Waldorf Institute, Sunbridge, because it is the Sunbridge, the Rainbow Sunbridge. This is the background for the name of Sunbridge College.

You will see the Rainbow Bridge with a being crossing the bridge from one side to another. You will be familiar with this from Goethe's famous poem "The Green Snake and the Beautiful Lily." It is the process that one lives in a very delicate aspect of nature meditatively until one has in consciousness, not of the snake, but the rainbow. And the rainbow consciousness is a next step in meditative work. If you think of the rainbow made between the warmth, the air, the light, and the darkness, you have there a highly refined state in nature. This is something that can be somewhat reproduced in meditative consciousness. For this is the crossing of the rainbow bridge through nature. This is not a mystical path; this is an occult path where one has what is in nature become the basis for one's meditative work that one comes to through inner experiences that are objectively mystical. It is called occult mysticism. This is a picture of the effort to cross that bridge, from this side to the other side. The rainbow leads one there. It is an amazing creation of the moment, as you know, and that is true in meditative consciousness.

You have to think that Pfeiffer was not a trained painter. If you saw some of his early things, you would see he had to practice, and this is not a usual artistic expression. There is a tremendous artistry in what he has done; quite unique.

Painting 6

This path of meditation, from the sun of the heavens to the sun of the earth, is also called a heart meditative path. This is a picture of the meditating soul and experiences of the heart that is, of course, no usual anatomical drawing. But there is the effort here, heading towards an exact fantasy of the etheric heart, sometimes called the fifth chamber. This is the heart in systole. You will see the dove above; you will see the hands below.

Here you see an eye in the middle of the yellow and two hands. These are the hands of God, as it were, but it is also an expression of experiencing one's own hands as etheric existences. That is when the heart enters the hands. I recall the hand-heart meditation, the heart in systole and diastole. You will see the hand and you will see the eye of God above and you will see the birds, like the dove, the holy spirit being present in this. One can say, this is the path of the heart. It is very typical of the path of the Rosicrucian.

Dr. Pfeiffer was a Rosicrucian, also in the sense that Rosicrucians don't go around selling themselves. He is well-known world over by people but for a man to be as productive as he was and as unknown as he is, I would say is typical of a real Rosicrucian striver.

Painting 7

Next is the heart in diastole where, as it were, God has been taken in and you see the dove is close to the heart. The heart is enlarged. The heart is taking in the world, like the hands that really are of an etheric nature taking in the world. For those that want to help people, that is what one needs, the heart and the hands. It is an extension of our physical heart but you can see our healing hands. You see the dove in contraction and relaxation or in the breathing of the heart. The symbol of the bird, of course, means that the search is for the spirit that is active in a meditative state. You can say this is the path of the heart.

Painting 8

Now this is a picture of, as it were, going up into the heights and again into the waters of the earth. You will see the colors and the whole coloring is a little darker than what you have with the heart. The heart-meditative activity has more light in it. This, when one contrasts where one has to go on earth, the actual physical earth, then you can come more to the mountain and then the depths of the mountain and then again in the earth, in the depths of the earth.

So it is meditatively, as it were, going where one might go when one takes a spiritual walk up the mountain and into the depths that lie on the mountain. Then you will see this, like you saw the first, where you had the sun and the running water and the earth, (the dry) earth. This is all part of a spiritual path. And it is also not that you just continue one meditative activity after another; one often has to come and return and then make that repeat. So you will see a repeat of the scene of the heights and the depths.

Painting 9

You can say that this is now a picture within the chambers of the earth, with beings that are busy with changes that are going on, as it were - a cauldron in the depths of the earth. It is an alchemic theme where the depths of the earth become the experience of alchemic events. Think that Dr. Pfeiffer not only was busy meditatively, but in the laboratory. He had somebody that worked with him and that was Erika Sabarth. She was deeply ingrained with enthusiasm for a new alchemy. There are few people that have devoted themselves to laboratory work with the intent of finding the spirit in matter as is true of Erika. I would say she understood where Pfeiffer was going. There were other ladies in the laboratory that adored him, but didn't understand and so relationships were not always easy.

Painting 10

The next is a painting I would call a Rosicrucian garden. Start with the garden as a kind of a picture of a flower garden. You see the foxglove, and you will notice the kind of elemental beings that invest the poisonous plant. The poisonous plant was often of interest to the Rosicrucian meditant because of its poison that attracted a spiritual being with a certain concentration so it can be seen, where it is not always seen with a normal flower.

You see, it is an otherworldly view of this world. And the otherworldly comes out of meditative effort, not just sitting waiting for things to happen. You don't paint these things out of flights of one's imagination.

Painting 11

This is a scene where the Egyptian cultural period stands behind it. You will see a pyramid in the situation and then you see a dragon-like being. You see the cross to the sunlight and the lightning in the depths of the earth. I would say this is a Christian theme but you can say it is also an Osiris/Isis theme. It belongs very much to the Rosicrucian meditant where the alchemist and alchemy become important, and the hermitic path, the Egyptian path, is very much that of chemistry and alchemy. It is held that alchemy was born in Egypt with the culture of Hermes. One is talking 3000 BC. Now the question is, what appears in consciousness when one begins to have history play itself out in one's meditation? It is coming in through the domain where history plays itself out in meditative effort.

Painting 12

This is coming to modern times and many will be familiar with a building that was built called the first Goetheanum. The pillars are around a central altar. The three figures there are very likely representative of Parsival (yellow), Christian Rosencreutz (red) and Rudolf Steiner (blue). These three individuals work together very intensely. Often one talks about one, but if you look into the spiritual history of things, you will see Mani Parsival, Christian Rosencreutz and if you are careful, you can find traces of Rudolf Steiner. What is here is that one is not in nature, but one is within a building that has been built so that individuals can have meditative experiences in that auditorium and see what is happening. The idea and importance of the First Goetheanum was to create, as it were, a meditative space. He named these three because there are indications from individuals that these were the three that were very important in trying to found a society of human beings, an Anthroposophical Society, where an openness and freedom and multifarious approach to life is possible. Always three represent very, very different revelations in history, if you go into occult history.

This is not a Rosicrucian path but the path that Rudolf Steiner tried to help so that those in the building could have the experience of the Grail, that means of substance. I would say that is a Rosicrucian-Anthroposophical path. Those forms that you have, the architraves, they exist in the world, and they exist where gradually the physical and the etheric meet when there is effort at structuring, building so individuals can have the experiences, not in nature but by an artistic creation.

When you look at the First Goetheanum, it wasn't exactly something Rudolf Steiner created out of his head. It is something that stands there and is in, as it were, the spiritual world. What one can say is it became very tangible for him when a young child was killed in Dornach while they were building the building. He pointed out that the soul of this child was very important to the architectural form that he then could bring over and try to put into a building.

Painting 13

Here you go out of the building once more. You are now not so much in the earthly domain, but more in the atmosphere, more in the airy, the wind and the air, an airy domain. The domain of the breath and there one can see what a whirlwind of activity can come meditatively when one tries to get to where our winds blow and can carry us away at times if they blow hard enough. This does not mean that through meditation one comes into the area where the air process is so dynamic that one experiences the actual rush of air in the atmosphere. I would say this is the meditation on our atmosphere, experienced through meditation.

Painting 14

I would say this is the alchemy of our atmosphere and cosmos. You can see the pillars that were in the Goetheanum. They are not just found there but they are found on a meditative path, and they belong to the path into the atmosphere where we have our planets and sun and moon and stars and so on. Here you can see, as it were, the gold of the sun, but it is alchemic gold; it is the metal in a warmth state that one experiences on a meditative path with meditative effort. You can see the ladies that move the planetary world. They are often called the seven liberal planetary arts. Moses experienced them in his meditation as one of the daughters of Jethro. I think even if one had a right "artistic fantasy" it would be difficult to come up with this type of content. The delicateness, the transparency of the colors and the activity in the pictures is rather astounding.

Painting 15

This, I would say, is a painting of the Grail experience in consciousness where a higher spiritual being is with the meditant, and he experiences earthliness as a vessel. You see the vessel there. That means the earth is a vessel for spiritual beingness. The earth becomes, as it were, the chalice in which spiritual beings can then work to create transformations. Notice the movement in the whole, how un-static that is. One has to catch what is in consciousness with a certain immediacy and when one is painting it, to have to be able to return to it again and again.

You see the physiognomy in the upper corner? You have a sense that in meditative work Pfeiffer had a certain consciousness of being overseen by spiritual beings. The question is, what kind of spiritual beings? I would say the next paintings are spiritual beings that have been read about here very regularly for the last forty years. These are the archangels connected with the seasons.

Painting 16

I would suggest that this is a rendering of Gabriel, well known to Moses and well known in the Rosicrucian work with the seasons. He is the archangel of Winter. You see this kind of gesture of carrying a being. It is almost like a child. If you watch the eyes in these next pictures, you will see how different each one is. Again, this is meditatively experienced; this is not that one is trying to copy something that is going on in a season. To walk with the archangel is actually meant to be a more common experience. And that is also why Rudolf Steiner gave the lectures, *The Four Seasons and the Archangels*, so we could become familiar with these beings.

Painting 17

Now you see the difference; you do not have green eyes, but you have receding oranges; the individuality is not so much there as is the movement around the spiritual beings. If you look, you will see how the hands are held, just in the area of the larynx so that the word can become, I would say, healing. This is the being of Mercury or Raphael. You can see this kind of delicate tending of the area, in which the larynx is located, so that the spoken word can be a healing word. Then you could say this is on the way to the word that is healed. The word process is what points to the future. You will notice it is not going into mountains or into caves. The whole perspective lies in what comes from this spoken word, from just this area of our makeup. That will be our future. Prayerful words you could say. You see how the hands are held. You can almost hear them. You can see how different this is from the previous archangel being. One would have to take the movement, the gesture, the quality that is portrayed here that then meets with one beyond the picture to meditative consciousness.

I would say that one has a person here, Ehrenfried Pfeiffer, who worked in other places for a good number of years, then came here (Spring Valley, now Chestnut Ridge) in the latter part of the forties, living here more or less until the end of his life. He lectured every other weekend. This is a very serious individual, and I think invested the whole area, including the earth being here, with an elemental quality that often makes people come and say, "Oh, there is something here." I would say it is because people are working in this way meditatively. This is a person that is an outstanding example. We are talking about healing. Raphael is the archangel of the healer. It is a very delicate gesture that holds the larynx, that which is necessary for the word. The healing word is the secret of Raphael.

Painting 18

See the sword here, down here the snake and dragon and there you have Michael. With his other hand, he is pointing to the being up above. Look at the gaze. It is again a different gesture with the eyes. As it were, in meditative work, dealing with one's lower nature in order to make further steps.

In my musings on this painting, I had to consider that this picture was influenced by Uriel as well as Michael. You see that the lightening stroke, the gesture, the silent Uriel and something that works strongly into the depths, let us say of substance. Dr. Pfeiffer lived with these kinds of things and individuals were not aware that this was the case. If I showed you the pictures of the handling of garbage in California you would wonder how a man like that could be making compost out of garbage and painting pictures like this. He gave a formula for a preparation that Maggie Selke made and prepared here in Threefold. He gave her a kind of altered meditative work to do every Sunday, which she did for forty years. And that went out with the compost preparation, with the starter.

Painting 19

It is a beautiful flower, isn't it? It is a flower of the heart. With that one can hear things. Musicians sometimes tell how strongly they experience music rising from within the heart. That is all a silent process,

There was a lot of talk about the lotus flowers when this was being painted. I would suggest this is a metamorphosis of what you have with the heart paintings where you have this wonderful flower. It is so delicate and so transparent: as it were, the eyes to the other world. When you get to this kind of a painting one hardly is in touch with the physical world. It is then into another world. I would say that world, that touches into it belongs to the heart insofar as it belongs to conscience. Our conscience organ is our heart. Our heart is built in such a way that it is the mirror for what we do, and when we search our soul and/or conscience, the mirror, the exacting mirror, is our heart. It is connected with the living soul nature of the heart, I would say, the astral or the lotus organ. It takes one to an archangel.

Painting 20

Here you see the archangel is silent and asks that one is silent. You will see the gesture is silent. There one is silent in the word so that the heart can actually speak the conscience. This is a rendering, I would say, of Uriel. You have a painted picture of Uriel over the mailboxes in Hill Top House. Very few people have painted pictures of Uriel, and this is rather unusual. You see this silence in the spirit and the slowing course of the warmth and heat of the individual spirit. You can see how the fire warmth becomes ego warmth while support for the individual is peace and quiet. It is the fire of enthusiasm, the spiritual enthusiasm. Flames of the heart, they are speaking the truth and the proper judgment. And Uriel is the archangel very much connected with that. He is the mid-summer archangel. And this is all meditatively expressed.

You will notice the eyes on the side and that is always a Rosicrucian symbol, not only what is on our dollar bill, but a symbolical rendering of the eyes of God. So it takes one to another level of existence, a higher domain, and there one can say, one is silenced so that one can come to one's true conscience and, as it were, then to God. It is carried by the heart, and it comes with the evolution of heart consciousness. The Rosicrucian does not think you can just sit down and have God at your side. It is a long path to tread and a lot of work to do to hear the words that belong to the domain of God. One needs a lot of angelic help to get to know God in meditative consciousness, not because one is reading somebody else's experiences. Those fires are very important. It is often overlooked, the kind of inner fire that has to come with meditative work so that one is really fired and carried by the warmth in meditation.

Painting 21

This picture has always puzzled me. This is the triangle, again symbolically representative of the triune spiritual godly element. That is another step in meditativeness, to come to the triunity of existence. This is a real wrestling of one's being, of one's conscience. In meditative consciousness, of course, a person just doesn't hold it there and then make a picture. One has to return to the meditative state again and again and again. So you ask how long it takes to paint such a picture. I would say the person has to be able to return to what comes in his soul so that he can continue to paint.

I think what is interesting is that this picture is not delicate at all. It is real wrestling of one's being, one's conscience. This is the end of the journey.